Table of Contents
1. **Foundational Beliefs**
    - The Nature of God
    - Jesus Christ
    - The Holy Spirit
    - The Bible
2. **Personal Growth and Discipleship**
    - Prayer
    - Worship
    - Faith and Trust in God
    - Holiness and Sanctification
    - Spiritual Disciplines
3. **Community and Relationships**
    - Church
    - Evangelism and Mission
    - Christian Community and Fellowship
4. **Moral and Ethical Living**
    - Christian Ethics
    - Love and Compassion
    - Forgiveness and Reconciliation
5. **Practical Christian Living**
    - Stewardship
    - Work and Vocation
    - Family Life
6. **Apologetics and Defending the Faith**
    - Apologetics
    - Worldview
7. **Suffering and Perseverance**
    - Suffering and Trials
    - Spiritual Warfare
8. **Future Hope**
    - Eschatology
9. **Living Out the Faith**
    - Living Out the Gospel
10. **Conclusion**
    - Continuous Growth
11. **Chapter Eleven**

- Living Out the Gospel

12 .**Chapter Twelve**
- Overcoming Struggles

CHAPTER ONE: FOUNDATIONAL BELIEFS

The Nature of God

Understanding the nature of God is fundamental to the Christian faith. God is the creator of the universe and everything in it. He is eternal, omnipotent, omniscient, and omnipresent. Here are some key attributes and scriptural references:

1. **Eternal**: God has no beginning and no end. He always was and always will be.

    - **Scripture**: "Before the mountains were born or you brought forth the whole world, from everlasting to everlasting you are God." (Psalm 90:2)

2. **Omnipotent**: God is all-powerful and capable of doing anything that is consistent with His nature.

    - **Scripture**: "I am the Lord, the God of all mankind. Is anything too hard for me?" (Jeremiah 32:27)

3. **Omniscient**: God is all-knowing. He knows everything about everyone and everything.

    - **Scripture**: "Great is our Lord and mighty in power; his understanding has no limit." (Psalm 147:5)

4. **Omnipresent**: God is present everywhere at all times.

    - **Scripture**: "Where can I go from your Spirit? Where can

I flee from your presence?" (Psalm 139:7)
5. **Loving**: God's love is unconditional and everlasting.
    - **Scripture**: "Whoever does not love does not know God, because God is love." (1 John 4:8)
6. **Holy**: God is perfect and pure, without any sin.
    - **Scripture**: "Holy, holy, holy is the Lord Almighty; the whole earth is full of his glory." (Isaiah 6:3)

Instructions for Personal Study:

- Reflect on these attributes of God and how they impact your understanding of Him.
- Pray, asking God to reveal more of His nature to you.
- Meditate on the scriptures provided.

Jesus Christ

Jesus Christ is central to Christianity. He is the Son of God who came to earth to save humanity from sin. Here are essential aspects to understand:

1. **Incarnation**: Jesus, though fully God, became fully human.
    - **Scripture**: "The Word became flesh and made his dwelling among us. We have seen his glory, the glory of the one and only Son, who came from the Father, full of grace and truth." (John 1:14)
2. **Life and Teachings**: Jesus lived a sinless life and taught about the Kingdom of God.
    - **Scripture**: "Jesus went throughout Galilee, teaching in their synagogues, proclaiming the good news of the kingdom, and healing every disease and sickness among the people." (Matthew 4:23)
3. **Death and Resurrection**: Jesus died on the cross for our sins and rose from the dead, defeating death.
    - **Scripture**: "He was delivered over to death for our

sins and was raised to life for our justification." (Romans 4:25)

4. **Ascension**: Jesus ascended to heaven and is seated at the right hand of the Father.

    ◦ **Scripture**: "After he said this, he was taken up before their very eyes, and a cloud hid him from their sight." (Acts 1:9)

Instructions for Personal Study:

- Read the Gospels (Matthew, Mark, Luke, and John) to learn more about Jesus' life and teachings.
- Consider how Jesus' sacrifice impacts your life.
- Spend time in prayer, thanking Jesus for His sacrifice and asking for a deeper understanding of His teachings.

The Holy Spirit

The Holy Spirit is the third person of the Trinity and plays an essential role in the life of a believer.

1. **Presence**: The Holy Spirit dwells within believers.

    ◦ **Scripture**: "Do you not know that your bodies are temples of the Holy Spirit, who is in you, whom you have received from God?" (1 Corinthians 6:19)

2. **Guide and Comforter**: The Holy Spirit guides believers and provides comfort.

    ◦ **Scripture**: "But the Advocate, the Holy Spirit, whom the Father will send in my name, will teach you all things and will remind you of everything I have said to you." (John 14:26)

3. **Empowerment**: The Holy Spirit empowers believers to live a godly life and to witness to others.

    ◦ **Scripture**: "But you will receive power when the Holy Spirit comes on you; and you will be my witnesses in Jerusalem, and in all Judea and Samaria, and to the ends of the earth." (Acts 1:8)

Instructions for Personal Study:

- Pray and ask the Holy Spirit to fill you and guide you in all aspects of your life.
- Seek to understand the gifts of the Spirit and how they can be used in your life (see 1 Corinthians 12).
- Reflect on how the Holy Spirit has worked in your life and share your experiences with others.

The Bible

The Bible is the inspired word of God and is essential for knowing God's will and truth.

1. **Inspiration**: The Bible is God-breathed and authoritative.

    - **Scripture**: "All Scripture is God-breathed and is useful for teaching, rebuking, correcting and training in righteousness." (2 Timothy 3:16)

2. **Purpose**: The Bible teaches us about God, gives instructions for living, and provides encouragement.

    - **Scripture**: "Your word is a lamp for my feet, a light on my path." (Psalm 119:105)

3. **Truth**: The Bible is true and reliable.

    - **Scripture**: "Sanctify them by the truth; your word is truth." (John 17:17)

Instructions for Personal Study:

- Set aside regular time each day to read and meditate on the Bible.
- Memorize key verses that speak to your heart and circumstances.
- Use a study guide or join a Bible study group to deepen your understanding of the scriptures.

Conclusion

Understanding the foundational beliefs of Christianity is crucial for a strong faith. By knowing the nature of God, the role of Jesus Christ, the work of the Holy Spirit, and the importance of the Bible, you build a solid base for your spiritual journey.

Reflection and Application:

- Reflect on how each of these foundational beliefs has impacted your faith.
- Write down any questions you have and seek answers through prayer, scripture, or discussion with a trusted mentor or pastor.
- Apply these truths to your daily life, striving to grow closer to God.

Remember, this journey is ongoing. Continue to seek God and deepen your understanding of these foundational beliefs.

CHAPTER TWO: PERSONAL GROWTH AND DISCIPLESHIP

Prayer

Prayer is a fundamental practice for personal growth and discipleship. It is our direct line of communication with God and plays a crucial role in deepening our relationship with Him.

1. **Purpose of Prayer**: Prayer allows us to communicate with God, express our needs, and align our will with His.
    - **Scripture**: "Do not be anxious about anything, but in every situation, by prayer and petition, with thanksgiving, present your requests to God." (Philippians 4:6)
2. **Types of Prayer**: There are various types of prayer, including adoration, confession, thanksgiving, and supplication (ACTS).
    - **Adoration**: Praising God for who He is.
    - **Confession**: Admitting our sins and asking for forgiveness.
    - **Thanksgiving**: Expressing gratitude for God's blessings.
    - **Supplication**: Asking God for our needs and the needs of others.
3. **Jesus' Example**: Jesus often withdrew to pray, showing us the importance of regular, intentional prayer.

- **Scripture**: "But Jesus often withdrew to lonely places and prayed." (Luke 5:16)

Instructions for Personal Study:

- Set aside a specific time each day for prayer.
- Use the ACTS model to guide your prayers.
- Keep a prayer journal to track your requests and note how God answers them.

Worship

Worship is a vital part of personal growth and discipleship. It is an expression of our love and reverence for God.

1. **Definition of Worship**: Worship involves giving God the glory and honor He deserves, both individually and collectively.
   - **Scripture**: "Ascribe to the Lord the glory due his name; worship the Lord in the splendor of his holiness." (Psalm 29:2)
2. **Forms of Worship**: Worship can take many forms, including singing, praying, reading scripture, and serving others.
   - **Scripture**: "Come, let us bow down in worship, let us kneel before the Lord our Maker." (Psalm 95:6)
3. **Heart of Worship**: True worship comes from the heart and is not merely about external actions.
   - **Scripture**: "God is spirit, and his worshipers must worship in the Spirit and in truth." (John 4:24)

Instructions for Personal Study:

- Engage in regular personal worship times through prayer, singing, and reading scripture.
- Attend corporate worship services to join with others in praising God.
- Reflect on your heart's attitude during worship and seek to worship God in spirit and truth.

Faith and Trust in God

Having faith and trust in God is crucial for spiritual growth. It involves believing in His promises and relying on Him in all circumstances.

1. **Definition of Faith**: Faith is the assurance of things hoped for and the conviction of things not seen.
   - **Scripture**: "Now faith is confidence in what we hope for and assurance about what we do not see." (Hebrews 11:1)
2. **Living by Faith**: Faith requires us to trust God's plan, even when we do not understand it.
   - **Scripture**: "Trust in the Lord with all your heart and lean not on your own understanding." (Proverbs 3:5)
3. **Examples of Faith**: The Bible is full of examples of individuals who demonstrated great faith, such as Abraham, Moses, and David.
   - **Scripture**: "By faith Abraham, when called to go to a place he would later receive as his inheritance, obeyed and went, even though he did not know where he was going." (Hebrews 11:8)

Instructions for Personal Study:

- Reflect on areas in your life where you need to trust God more.
- Study the lives of biblical characters who exhibited strong faith.
- Pray for increased faith and trust in God's plans.

Holiness and Sanctification

Holiness and sanctification are processes of becoming more like Christ, set apart for God's purposes.

1. **Holiness**: God calls us to live holy lives, set apart from sin.
   - **Scripture**: "But just as he who called you is holy, so be holy in all you do; for it is written: 'Be holy, because I am

holy.'" (1 Peter 1:15-16)
2. **Sanctification**: This is the process of being made holy, which involves spiritual growth and maturity.

    - **Scripture**: "For this is the will of God, your sanctification." (1 Thessalonians 4:3)
3. **Role of the Holy Spirit**: The Holy Spirit works within us to transform us into the image of Christ.

    - **Scripture**: "And we all, who with unveiled faces contemplate the Lord's glory, are being transformed into his image with ever-increasing glory, which comes from the Lord, who is the Spirit." (2 Corinthians 3:18)

Instructions for Personal Study:

- Examine your life for areas that need purification and surrender them to God.
- Pray for the Holy Spirit to guide and transform you.
- Commit to regular Bible study and prayer to grow in holiness.

Spiritual Disciplines

Spiritual disciplines are practices that help us grow in our faith and become more like Christ.

1. **Bible Reading**: Regularly reading and studying the Bible is essential for spiritual growth.

    - **Scripture**: "Your word is a lamp for my feet, a light on my path." (Psalm 119:105)
2. **Prayer**: Daily communication with God through prayer strengthens our relationship with Him.

    - **Scripture**: "Pray continually." (1 Thessalonians 5:17)
3. **Fasting**: Fasting helps us to focus on God and seek His will.

    - **Scripture**: "But when you fast, put oil on your head and wash your face, so that it will not be obvious to others that you are fasting, but only to your Father, who

is unseen; and your Father, who sees what is done in secret, will reward you." (Matthew 6:17-18)
4. **Service**: Serving others is a practical way to demonstrate Christ's love.

    ○ **Scripture**: "Each of you should use whatever gift you have received to serve others, as faithful stewards of God's grace in its various forms." (1 Peter 4:10)

Instructions for Personal Study:

- Develop a daily routine that includes Bible reading, prayer, and other spiritual disciplines.
- Set specific goals for how you will incorporate these practices into your life.
- Reflect on the impact of these disciplines on your spiritual growth and make adjustments as needed.

Community and Relationships

Christianity is not a solitary journey; it involves being part of a community and building relationships with others.

1. **Importance of Community**: Being part of a Christian community provides support, encouragement, and accountability.

    ○ **Scripture**: "And let us consider how we may spur one another on toward love and good deeds, not giving up meeting together, as some are in the habit of doing, but encouraging one another." (Hebrews 10:24-25)

2. **Building Relationships**: Forming meaningful relationships with other believers helps us to grow and serve together.

    ○ **Scripture**: "As iron sharpens iron, so one person sharpens another." (Proverbs 27:17)

3. **Serving in Community**: Serving within a community helps to meet the needs of others and fulfill God's purposes.

    ○ **Scripture**: "Carry each other's burdens, and in this way

you will fulfill the law of Christ." (Galatians 6:2)
Instructions for Personal Study:

- Get involved in a local church or small group.
- Build and nurture relationships with other believers.
- Look for opportunities to serve within your community and support others in their faith journey.

Conclusion

Personal growth and discipleship involve a commitment to prayer, worship, faith, holiness, spiritual disciplines, and community. By focusing on these areas, you can deepen your relationship with God and become more like Christ.

Reflection and Application:

- Reflect on each aspect of personal growth and discipleship.
- Identify specific actions you can take to grow in each area.
- Pray for God's guidance and strength as you commit to these practices.

Remember, personal growth and discipleship are lifelong journeys. Continue to seek God and strive to grow in your faith every day.

CHAPTER THREE: FAITH AND TRUST IN GOD

Faith and Trust in God

Having faith and trust in God is essential for a vibrant Christian life. It means believing in God's promises and relying on Him in every circumstance.

1. **Definition of Faith**: Faith is confidence in what we hope for and assurance about what we do not see.
    - **Scripture**: "Now faith is confidence in what we hope for and assurance about what we do not see." (Hebrews 11:1)
2. **Living by Faith**: Living by faith means trusting God's plan even when we do not understand it.
    - **Scripture**: "For we live by faith, not by sight." (2 Corinthians 5:7)
3. **Faith in Action**: Faith is demonstrated through actions. True faith impacts our decisions and behaviors.
    - **Scripture**: "In the same way, faith by itself, if it is not accompanied by action, is dead." (James 2:17)

Instructions for Personal Study:

- Reflect on areas in your life where you need to exercise more faith.
- Pray for increased faith and the courage to trust God in all

circumstances.
- Read Hebrews 11, which lists many examples of faith from the Bible.

Holiness and Sanctification

Holiness and sanctification are about becoming more like Jesus, setting ourselves apart for God's purposes.

1. **Call to Holiness**: God calls us to live holy lives, reflecting His purity and righteousness.
    - **Scripture**: "But just as he who called you is holy, so be holy in all you do; for it is written: 'Be holy, because I am holy.'" (1 Peter 1:15-16)
2. **Sanctification Process**: Sanctification is the ongoing process of being made holy, involving spiritual growth and maturity.
    - **Scripture**: "For this is the will of God, your sanctification." (1 Thessalonians 4:3)
3. **Role of the Holy Spirit**: The Holy Spirit works within us to transform us into the image of Christ.
    - **Scripture**: "And we all, who with unveiled faces contemplate the Lord's glory, are being transformed into his image with ever-increasing glory, which comes from the Lord, who is the Spirit." (2 Corinthians 3:18)

Instructions for Personal Study:

- Regularly examine your life and identify areas that need purification.
- Pray for the Holy Spirit to guide and transform you.
- Commit to regular Bible study and prayer to grow in holiness.

Spiritual Disciplines

Spiritual disciplines are practices that help us grow in our faith and become more like Christ.

1. **Bible Reading**: Regularly reading and studying the Bible is essential for spiritual growth.

- **Scripture**: "Your word is a lamp for my feet, a light on my path." (Psalm 119:105)
2. **Prayer**: Daily communication with God through prayer strengthens our relationship with Him.
    - **Scripture**: "Pray continually." (1 Thessalonians 5:17)
3. **Fasting**: Fasting helps us focus on God and seek His will.
    - **Scripture**: "But when you fast, put oil on your head and wash your face, so that it will not be obvious to others that you are fasting, but only to your Father, who is unseen; and your Father, who sees what is done in secret, will reward you." (Matthew 6:17-18)
4. **Service**: Serving others is a practical way to demonstrate Christ's love.
    - **Scripture**: "Each of you should use whatever gift you have received to serve others, as faithful stewards of God's grace in its various forms." (1 Peter 4:10)

Instructions for Personal Study:

- Develop a daily routine that includes Bible reading, prayer, and other spiritual disciplines.
- Set specific goals for how you will incorporate these practices into your life.
- Reflect on the impact of these disciplines on your spiritual growth and make adjustments as needed.

Community and Relationships

Christianity is not a solitary journey; it involves being part of a community and building relationships with others.

1. **Importance of Community**: Being part of a Christian community provides support, encouragement, and accountability.
    - **Scripture**: "And let us consider how we may spur one another on toward love and good deeds, not giving up meeting together, as some are in the habit of doing, but

encouraging one another." (Hebrews 10:24-25)
2. **Building Relationships**: Forming meaningful relationships with other believers helps us to grow and serve together.

    ◦ **Scripture**: "As iron sharpens iron, so one person sharpens another." (Proverbs 27:17)
3. **Serving in Community**: Serving within a community helps to meet the needs of others and fulfill God's purposes.

    ◦ **Scripture**: "Carry each other's burdens, and in this way you will fulfill the law of Christ." (Galatians 6:2)

Instructions for Personal Study:

- Get involved in a local church or small group.
- Build and nurture relationships with other believers.
- Look for opportunities to serve within your community and support others in their faith journey.

Conclusion

Personal growth and discipleship involve a commitment to prayer, worship, faith, holiness, spiritual disciplines, and community. By focusing on these areas, you can deepen your relationship with God and become more like Christ.

Reflection and Application:

- Reflect on each aspect of personal growth and discipleship.
- Identify specific actions you can take to grow in each area.
- Pray for God's guidance and strength as you commit to these practices.

Remember, personal growth and discipleship are lifelong journeys. Continue to seek God and strive to grow in your faith every day.

CHAPTER FOUR: CHURCH

Evangelism and Mission

Evangelism and mission are essential parts of the Christian faith, involving sharing the gospel and serving others.

1. **Great Commission**: Jesus commands us to spread the gospel and make disciples of all nations.
    - **Scripture**: "Therefore go and make disciples of all nations, baptizing them in the name of the Father and of the Son and of the Holy Spirit." (Matthew 28:19)
2. **Being a Witness**: We are called to be witnesses for Christ in our daily lives.
    - **Scripture**: "But you will receive power when the Holy Spirit comes on you; and you will be my witnesses in Jerusalem, and in all Judea and Samaria, and to the ends of the earth." (Acts 1:8)
3. **Serving Others**: Mission work involves serving others and meeting their physical and spiritual needs.
    - **Scripture**: "The King will reply, 'Truly I tell you, whatever you did for one of the least of these brothers and sisters of mine, you did for me.'" (Matthew 25:40)

Instructions for Personal Study:

- Reflect on how you can be a witness for Christ in your daily life.
- Look for opportunities to share the gospel with others.

- Get involved in mission projects or service opportunities through your church or community.

Christian Community and Fellowship

Being part of a Christian community is vital for spiritual growth and support.

1. **Importance of Fellowship**: Fellowship with other believers provides encouragement and accountability.
    - **Scripture**: "They devoted themselves to the apostles' teaching and to fellowship, to the breaking of bread and to prayer." (Acts 2:42)
2. **Building Relationships**: Strong relationships within the Christian community help us to grow and serve together.
    - **Scripture**: "As iron sharpens iron, so one person sharpens another." (Proverbs 27:17)
3. **Serving One Another**: We are called to serve each other within the community of believers.
    - **Scripture**: "Carry each other's burdens, and in this way you will fulfill the law of Christ." (Galatians 6:2)

Instructions for Personal Study:

- Engage in regular fellowship with other believers through church activities and small groups.
- Build and nurture meaningful relationships within your Christian community.
- Look for ways to serve and support others in your community.

Moral and Ethical Living

Living a life that reflects Christ involves adhering to moral and ethical standards as outlined in the Bible.

1. **Biblical Standards**: The Bible provides clear guidelines for moral and ethical behavior.
    - **Scripture**: "Your word is a lamp for my feet, a light on my

path." (Psalm 119:105)
2. **Integrity**: Living with integrity means being honest and upright in all our dealings.

   ◦ **Scripture**: "The integrity of the upright guides them, but the unfaithful are destroyed by their duplicity." (Proverbs 11:3)

3. **Love and Compassion**: We are called to love others and show compassion, reflecting Christ's love.

   ◦ **Scripture**: "Be kind and compassionate to one another, forgiving each other, just as in Christ God forgave you." (Ephesians 4:32)

Instructions for Personal Study:

- Reflect on your life and identify areas where you need to align more closely with biblical standards.
- Pray for the Holy Spirit to help you live with integrity and compassion.
- Seek to demonstrate Christ's love in all your interactions with others.

Conclusion

The church, evangelism, community, and ethical living are crucial aspects of the Christian faith. By engaging in these areas, we fulfill God's purposes and grow closer to Him.

Reflection and Application:

- Reflect on each aspect of church life and community involvement.
- Identify specific actions you can take to engage more fully in these areas.
- Pray for God's guidance and strength as you commit to these practices.

Remember, being part of a church and living out your faith in community is a lifelong journey. Continue to seek God and strive to grow in your faith every day.

CHAPTER FIVE: CHRISTIAN ETHICS

Love and Compassion

Love and compassion are at the heart of Christian ethics. Jesus emphasized the importance of loving God and loving others as the greatest commandments.

1. **Greatest Commandment**: Love God with all your heart, soul, and mind, and love your neighbor as yourself.
    - **Scripture**: "Jesus replied: 'Love the Lord your God with all your heart and with all your soul and with all your mind. This is the first and greatest commandment. And the second is like it: Love your neighbor as yourself.'" (Matthew 22:37-39)
2. **Example of Jesus**: Jesus demonstrated love and compassion throughout His ministry, healing the sick, feeding the hungry, and forgiving sins.
    - **Scripture**: "When Jesus landed and saw a large crowd, he had compassion on them and healed their sick." (Matthew 14:14)
3. **Call to Love**: We are called to love others as Christ loved us, sacrificially and unconditionally.
    - **Scripture**: "A new command I give you: Love one another. As I have loved you, so you must love one another." (John 13:34)

Instructions for Personal Study:

- Reflect on how you can show love and compassion to those around you.
- Pray for a heart that loves others as Christ loves you.
- Look for opportunities to serve and help others in practical ways.

Forgiveness and Reconciliation

Forgiveness and reconciliation are vital for maintaining healthy relationships and reflecting God's grace.

1. **Command to Forgive**: We are commanded to forgive others, just as God has forgiven us.
    - **Scripture**: "Bear with each other and forgive one another if any of you has a grievance against someone. Forgive as the Lord forgave you." (Colossians 3:13)
2. **Reconciliation**: We are called to seek reconciliation with those we have wronged or who have wronged us.
    - **Scripture**: "Therefore, if you are offering your gift at the altar and there remember that your brother or sister has something against you, leave your gift there in front of the altar. First go and be reconciled to them; then come and offer your gift." (Matthew 5:23-24)
3. **Example of Christ**: Jesus forgave those who crucified Him, setting the ultimate example of forgiveness.
    - **Scripture**: "Jesus said, 'Father, forgive them, for they do not know what they are doing.'" (Luke 23:34)

Instructions for Personal Study:

- Examine your heart for any unforgiveness and ask God to help you forgive.
- Seek reconciliation with those you have conflicts with.
- Pray for the ability to forgive as Christ forgave.

Practical Christian Living

Living out the Christian faith involves applying biblical principles to our daily lives.

1. **Honesty and Integrity**: Christians are called to live with honesty and integrity in all areas of life.
    - **Scripture**: "The integrity of the upright guides them, but the unfaithful are destroyed by their duplicity." (Proverbs 11:3)
2. **Humility**: Humility involves putting others before ourselves and recognizing our dependence on God.
    - **Scripture**: "Do nothing out of selfish ambition or vain conceit. Rather, in humility value others above yourselves." (Philippians 2:3)
3. **Service**: Serving others is a practical expression of our faith and love for God.
    - **Scripture**: "Each of you should use whatever gift you have received to serve others, as faithful stewards of God's grace in its various forms." (1 Peter 4:10)

Instructions for Personal Study:

- Reflect on how you can apply biblical principles to your daily life.
- Pray for the Holy Spirit to help you live with honesty, integrity, and humility.
- Look for opportunities to serve others in your community.

Conclusion

Christian ethics involves living out the principles of love, compassion, forgiveness, reconciliation, and practical Christian living. By following these guidelines, we can reflect Christ's character and make a positive impact on the world.

Reflection and Application:

- Reflect on each aspect of Christian ethics and how it applies to your life.
- Identify specific actions you can take to live out these

principles.
- Pray for God's guidance and strength as you commit to these practices.

Remember, living out Christian ethics is a lifelong journey. Continue to seek God and strive to grow in your faith every day.

CHAPTER SIX: STEWARDSHIP

Work and Vocation

Our work and vocation are areas where we can glorify God and serve others.

1. **Calling to Work**: God has given each of us unique gifts and talents to use in our work and vocation.
    - **Scripture**: "Whatever you do, work at it with all your heart, as working for the Lord, not for human masters." (Colossians 3:23)
2. **Integrity in Work**: We are called to work with integrity and excellence, reflecting God's character.
    - **Scripture**: "Whatever your hand finds to do, do it with all your might." (Ecclesiastes 9:10)
3. **Purpose in Work**: Our work should serve a greater purpose, contributing to the well-being of others and the advancement of God's kingdom.
    - **Scripture**: "For we are co-workers in God's service; you are God's field, God's building." (1 Corinthians 3:9)

Instructions for Personal Study:

- Reflect on your work and vocation and how you can use them to glorify God.
- Pray for the Holy Spirit to guide you in using your gifts and talents for His purposes.

- Look for ways to serve others and make a positive impact through your work.

Family Life

Family life is an essential part of Christian stewardship, involving loving and serving our family members.

1. **Love and Respect**: Husbands and wives are called to love and respect each other, reflecting Christ's love for the church.
    - **Scripture**: "Husbands, love your wives, just as Christ loved the church and gave himself up for her." (Ephesians 5:25)
    - **Scripture**: "However, each one of you also must love his wife as he loves himself, and the wife must respect her husband." (Ephesians 5:33)
2. **Raising Children**: Parents are called to raise their children in the knowledge and instruction of the Lord.
    - **Scripture**: "Fathers, do not exasperate your children; instead, bring them up in the training and instruction of the Lord." (Ephesians 6:4)
3. **Serving Your Family**: Serving and supporting our family members is a practical way to demonstrate God's love.
    - **Scripture**: "But if anyone does not provide for his relatives, and especially for members of his household, he has denied the faith and is worse than an unbeliever." (1 Timothy 5:8)

Instructions for Personal Study:

- Reflect on your role within your family and how you can better love and serve your family members.
- Pray for God's guidance and strength to fulfill your responsibilities within your family.
- Look for opportunities to support and encourage your family members in their faith journey.

Conclusion

Stewardship involves using our gifts, talents, and resources to glorify God and serve others in our work and family life.

Reflection and Application:

- Reflect on each aspect of stewardship and how it applies to your life.
- Identify specific actions you can take to use your gifts and talents for God's purposes.
- Pray for God's guidance and strength as you commit to these practices.

Remember, stewardship is a lifelong journey. Continue to seek God and strive to grow in your faith every day.

CHAPTER SEVEN: APOLOGETICS AND DEFENDING THE FAITH

Apologetics

Apologetics involves defending the Christian faith and providing reasons for our beliefs.

1. **Reason for Apologetics**: We are called to be prepared to give an answer for the hope that we have.
    - **Scripture**: "But in your hearts revere Christ as Lord. Always be prepared to give an answer to everyone who asks you to give the reason for the hope that you have. But do this with gentleness and respect." (1 Peter 3:15)
2. **Understanding Scripture**: Knowing the Bible is essential for effectively defending our faith.
    - **Scripture**: "All Scripture is God-breathed and is useful for teaching, rebuking, correcting and training in righteousness." (2 Timothy 3:16)
3. **Engaging with Others**: Apologetics involves engaging with others respectfully and lovingly.
    - **Scripture**: "Opponents must be gently instructed, in the hope that God will grant them repentance leading them to a knowledge of the truth." (2 Timothy 2:25)

Instructions for Personal Study:

- Study the Bible regularly to deepen your understanding of Scripture.
- Read books and resources on Christian apologetics to learn how to defend your faith.
- Practice explaining your beliefs to others with gentleness and respect.

Worldview

A Christian worldview involves seeing the world through the lens of biblical truth.

1. **Biblical Foundation**: A Christian worldview is based on the truths of the Bible.
    - **Scripture**: "For the word of the Lord is right and true; he is faithful in all he does." (Psalm 33:4)
2. **Impact on Life**: Our worldview affects how we live, make decisions, and interact with others.
    - **Scripture**: "Do not conform to the pattern of this world, but be transformed by the renewing of your mind. Then you will be able to test and approve what God's will is—his good, pleasing and perfect will." (Romans 12:2)
3. **Engaging Culture**: A Christian worldview involves engaging with culture and society in a way that reflects Christ's love and truth.
    - **Scripture**: "You are the light of the world. A town built on a hill cannot be hidden." (Matthew 5:14)

Instructions for Personal Study:

- Reflect on how your beliefs and values are influenced by a biblical worldview.
- Study the Bible to deepen your understanding of God's truth.
- Look for opportunities to engage with culture and society in a way that reflects your faith.

Conclusion

Apologetics and a Christian worldview are essential for defending our faith and living out our beliefs in the world.

Reflection and Application:

- Reflect on each aspect of apologetics and worldview and how they apply to your life.
- Identify specific actions you can take to defend your faith and live out a biblical worldview.
- Pray for God's guidance and strength as you commit to these practices.

Remember, defending your faith and living out a biblical worldview is a lifelong journey. Continue to seek God and strive to grow in your faith every day.

CHAPTER EIGHT: SUFFERING AND PERSEVERANCE

Suffering and Trials

Suffering and trials are a part of the Christian journey, but they can lead to growth and deeper faith.

1. **Purpose of Suffering**: Suffering can refine our faith and draw us closer to God.
    - **Scripture**: "Consider it pure joy, my brothers and sisters, whenever you face trials of many kinds, because you know that the testing of your faith produces perseverance." (James 1:2-3)
2. **God's Presence**: God is with us in our suffering and offers comfort and strength.
    - **Scripture**: "Even though I walk through the darkest valley, I will fear no evil, for you are with me; your rod and your staff, they comfort me." (Psalm 23:4)
3. **Hope in Suffering**: We have hope in the midst of suffering because of Christ's victory over sin and death.
    - **Scripture**: "I have told you these things, so that in me you may have peace. In this world you will have trouble. But take heart! I have overcome the world." (John 16:33)

Instructions for Personal Study:

- Reflect on past or present trials and how God has used them to grow your faith.
- Pray for strength and comfort in the midst of suffering.
- Study the lives of biblical characters who faced suffering and learn from their experiences.

Spiritual Warfare

Spiritual warfare involves the battle against spiritual forces of evil that seek to harm and hinder our faith.

1. **Reality of Spiritual Warfare**: The Bible teaches that we are in a spiritual battle.
    - **Scripture**: "For our struggle is not against flesh and blood, but against the rulers, against the authorities, against the powers of this dark world and against the spiritual forces of evil in the heavenly realms." (Ephesians 6:12)
2. **Armor of God**: God provides spiritual armor to protect and equip us for battle.
    - **Scripture**: "Put on the full armor of God, so that you can take your stand against the devil's schemes." (Ephesians 6:11)
3. **Victory in Christ**: We have victory over spiritual forces through Christ.
    - **Scripture**: "But thanks be to God! He gives us the victory through our Lord Jesus Christ." (1 Corinthians 15:57)

Instructions for Personal Study:

- Study Ephesians 6:10-18 to learn about the armor of God.
- Reflect on areas in your life where you need God's protection and strength.
- Pray for victory over spiritual battles and trust in God's power.

Conclusion

Suffering, trials, and spiritual warfare are part of the Christian journey, but they can lead to growth and deeper faith.

Reflection and Application:

- Reflect on each aspect of suffering and spiritual warfare and how they apply to your life.
- Identify specific actions you can take to trust God and seek His strength in difficult times.
- Pray for God's guidance and strength as you commit to these practices.

Remember, persevering through suffering and spiritual warfare is a lifelong journey. Continue to seek God and strive to grow in your faith every day.

CHAPTER NINE: FUTURE HOPE

Future Hope

As Christians, we have a future hope that is rooted in the promises of God and the victory of Jesus Christ.

1. **Hope of Resurrection**: We have the hope of resurrection and eternal life with Christ.
    - **Scripture**: "For the Lord himself will come down from heaven, with a loud command, with the voice of the archangel and with the trumpet call of God, and the dead in Christ will rise first." (1 Thessalonians 4:16)
2. **New Heaven and New Earth**: God promises a new heaven and a new earth where there will be no more suffering or pain.
    - **Scripture**: "Then I saw 'a new heaven and a new earth,' for the first heaven and the first earth had passed away, and there was no longer any sea." (Revelation 21:1)
3. **Eternal Glory**: Our present sufferings are not worth comparing with the glory that will be revealed in us.
    - **Scripture**: "I consider that our present sufferings are not worth comparing with the glory that will be revealed in us." (Romans 8:18)

Instructions for Personal Study:

- Reflect on the hope of resurrection and eternal life with Christ.

- Study Revelation 21-22 to learn about the new heaven and new earth.
- Pray for a deeper understanding of God's promises and future hope.

Conclusion

Our future hope as Christians is rooted in the promises of God and the victory of Jesus Christ.

Reflection and Application:

- Reflect on each aspect of future hope and how it applies to your life.
- Identify specific actions you can take to live in the light of this hope.
- Pray for God's guidance and strength as you commit to these practices.

Remember, holding on to future hope is a lifelong journey. Continue to seek God and strive to grow in your faith every day.

CHAPTER TEN: ESCHATOLOGY

Living Out the Faith

Living out our faith involves applying the truths of eschatology (the study of end times) to our daily lives.

1. **Expectation of Christ's Return**: We are called to live in expectation of Christ's return.

    - **Scripture**: "Therefore keep watch, because you do not know on what day your Lord will come." (Matthew 24:42)

2. **Holy Living**: Knowing that Christ will return motivates us to live holy and godly lives.

    - **Scripture**: "So then, dear friends, since you are looking forward to this, make every effort to be found spotless, blameless and at peace with him." (2 Peter 3:14)

3. **Spreading the Gospel**: We are called to spread the gospel and make disciples in light of Christ's return.

    - **Scripture**: "And this gospel of the kingdom will be preached in the whole world as a testimony to all nations, and then the end will come." (Matthew 24:14)

Instructions for Personal Study:

- Reflect on the expectation of Christ's return and how it impacts your daily life.
- Pray for the Holy Spirit to help you live a holy and godly life.

- Look for opportunities to share the gospel and make disciples.

Conclusion

Living out our faith involves applying the truths of eschatology to our daily lives, living in expectation of Christ's return, and spreading the gospel.

Reflection and Application:

- Reflect on each aspect of living out your faith and how it applies to your life.
- Identify specific actions you can take to live in expectation of Christ's return.
- Pray for God's guidance and strength as you commit to these practices.

Remember, living out your faith in light of eschatology is a lifelong journey. Continue to seek God and strive to grow in your faith every day.

CHAPTER ELEVEN: LIVING OUT THE GOSPEL

Conclusion: Continuous Growth

Living out the gospel involves a commitment to continuous growth in our faith and relationship with God.

1. **Ongoing Discipleship**: Discipleship is a lifelong journey of following Jesus and growing in our faith.

    ◦ **Scripture**: "Then he said to them all: 'Whoever wants to be my disciple must deny themselves and take up their cross daily and follow me.'" (Luke 9:23)
2. **Spiritual Growth**: We are called to grow in the grace and knowledge of our Lord and Savior Jesus Christ.

    ◦ **Scripture**: "But grow in the grace and knowledge of our Lord and Savior Jesus Christ. To him be glory both now and forever! Amen." (2 Peter 3:18)
3. **Perseverance**: We are encouraged to persevere in our faith and continue to seek God throughout our lives.

    ◦ **Scripture**: "Let us run with perseverance the race marked out for us, fixing our eyes on Jesus, the pioneer and perfecter of faith." (Hebrews 12:1-2)

Instructions for Personal Study:

- Reflect on your journey of discipleship and identify areas for growth.

- Pray for the Holy Spirit to guide and strengthen you in your walk with God.
- Commit to ongoing spiritual growth through regular Bible study, prayer, and fellowship with other believers.

Conclusion

Living out the gospel involves a commitment to continuous growth in our faith and relationship with God. By following Jesus, growing in grace and knowledge, and persevering in our faith, we can reflect Christ's character and make a positive impact on the world.

Reflection and Application:

- Reflect on each aspect of living out the gospel and how it applies to your life.
- Identify specific actions you can take to continue growing in your faith.
- Pray for God's guidance and strength as you commit to these practices.

Remember, living out the gospel and growing in your faith is a lifelong journey. Continue to seek God and strive to grow in your faith every day.

Continuous Growth

As we conclude this study, remember that continuous growth in your faith and relationship with God is essential. By committing to personal growth, discipleship, stewardship, apologetics, and living out the gospel, you can deepen your relationship with God and make a positive impact on the world.

Reflection and Application:

- Reflect on your journey and identify areas for growth.
- Commit to ongoing spiritual growth through regular Bible study, prayer, and fellowship with other believers.
- Pray for God's guidance and strength as you continue to seek Him and grow in your faith.

Remember, your journey of faith is a lifelong process. Continue to seek God, strive to grow in your faith, and live out the gospel every day.

40

CHAPTER TWELVE: OVERCOMING STRUGGLES

Christians face various struggles in life, including psychological, financial, physical, and spiritual challenges. This chapter aims to address these struggles and provide biblical encouragement and practical advice to help readers overcome them.

Psychological Struggles

Psychological struggles, such as anxiety, depression, and stress, can significantly impact one's mental health and overall well-being.

1. **Anxiety**: Many Christians struggle with anxiety, worrying about the future and the unknown.
    - **Scripture**: "Do not be anxious about anything, but in every situation, by prayer and petition, with thanksgiving, present your requests to God. And the peace of God, which transcends all understanding, will guard your hearts and your minds in Christ Jesus." (Philippians 4:6-7)

Advice:

- **Pray and Meditate**: Regularly pray and meditate on God's promises. Prayer can bring peace and reduce anxiety.
- **Trust in God**: Trust that God is in control and has a plan for your life. Let go of the need to control everything.
- **Seek Support**: Talk to a trusted friend, pastor, or counselor

about your anxieties.
2. **Depression**: Depression can make one feel hopeless and alone.
   ◦ **Scripture**: "The Lord is close to the brokenhearted and saves those who are crushed in spirit." (Psalm 34:18)

Advice:

- **Reach Out for Help**: Don't isolate yourself. Seek help from mental health professionals and lean on your support network.
- **Stay Connected to God**: Continue to pray, read the Bible, and stay connected to God, even when it feels difficult.
- **Engage in Community**: Stay involved in church and community activities. Being around supportive people can lift your spirits.

Financial Struggles

Financial difficulties can cause stress and strain on individuals and families.

1. **Lack of Provision**: Many Christians worry about not having enough to meet their needs.
   ◦ **Scripture**: "And my God will meet all your needs according to the riches of his glory in Christ Jesus." (Philippians 4:19)

Advice:

- **Budget Wisely**: Create and stick to a budget to manage your finances effectively.
- **Seek God's Provision**: Trust that God will provide for your needs. Pray for wisdom in managing your resources.
- **Avoid Debt**: Be cautious about accumulating debt. Try to live within your means and save for the future.

2. **Generosity**: Balancing financial struggles with the call to be generous can be challenging.
   ◦ **Scripture**: "Give, and it will be given to you. A good measure, pressed down, shaken together and running

over, will be poured into your lap. For with the measure you use, it will be measured to you." (Luke 6:38)

Advice:

- **Prioritize Giving**: Even in financial struggles, prioritize giving. Trust that God honors and blesses generosity.
- **Seek God's Guidance**: Pray for guidance on how to be a good steward of your finances and where to give.
- **Find Contentment**: Learn to be content with what you have, recognizing that true wealth is not measured by material possessions.

Physical Struggles

Physical struggles, such as illness and injury, can be discouraging and exhausting.

1. **Illness**: Facing health issues can be a significant challenge for many Christians.
    - **Scripture**: "Is anyone among you sick? Let them call the elders of the church to pray over them and anoint them with oil in the name of the Lord. And the prayer offered in faith will make the sick person well; the Lord will raise them up. If they have sinned, they will be forgiven." (James 5:14-15)

Advice:

- **Pray for Healing**: Seek prayer for healing from your church community and believe in God's power to heal.
- **Take Care of Your Body**: Follow medical advice and take care of your body through proper diet, exercise, and rest.
- **Find Strength in God**: Trust that God is with you in your suffering and can bring comfort and strength.

2. **Disability**: Living with a disability can present ongoing challenges.
    - **Scripture**: "But he said to me, 'My grace is sufficient for you, for my power is made perfect in weakness.' Therefore I will boast all the more gladly about my

weaknesses, so that Christ's power may rest on me." (2 Corinthians 12:9)

Advice:

- **Lean on God's Strength**: Recognize that God's strength is made perfect in your weakness.
- **Seek Support**: Don't hesitate to ask for help and seek support from your community.
- **Embrace Your Worth**: Remember that your value is not diminished by your physical abilities. You are precious in God's sight.

Spiritual Struggles

Spiritual struggles can include doubt, temptation, and feeling distant from God.

1. **Doubt**: Many Christians experience periods of doubt and questioning their faith.
    - **Scripture**: "Immediately the boy's father exclaimed, 'I do believe; help me overcome my unbelief!'" (Mark 9:24)

Advice:

- **Seek Answers**: Don't be afraid to ask questions and seek answers through prayer, Bible study, and conversations with mature Christians.
- **Be Honest with God**: Bring your doubts to God in prayer and ask for His help to strengthen your faith.
- **Stay Connected**: Stay involved in church and small groups where you can be encouraged and supported in your faith journey.

2. **Temptation**: Facing temptation is a common struggle for all Christians.
    - **Scripture**: "No temptation has overtaken you except what is common to mankind. And God is faithful; he will not let you be tempted beyond what you can bear. But when you are tempted, he will also provide a way out so that you can endure it." (1 Corinthians 10:13)

Advice:

- **Stay Vigilant**: Be aware of areas where you are prone to temptation and take steps to avoid them.
- **Rely on God's Strength**: Pray for strength to resist temptation and rely on God's power.
- **Accountability**: Have an accountability partner who can support you and help you stay strong in the face of temptation.

3. **Feeling Distant from God**: Sometimes, Christians feel spiritually dry or distant from God.
   - **Scripture**: "Draw near to God, and he will draw near to you." (James 4:8)

Advice:

- **Seek God Daily**: Make a habit of seeking God daily through prayer, Bible reading, and worship.
- **Engage in Community**: Stay connected with your church community, as fellowship can reignite your spiritual passion.
- **Persevere in Faith**: Continue to pursue God, even when you don't feel close to Him, trusting that He is with you.

Conclusion

Christians face various struggles, but God's Word provides encouragement and guidance for overcoming them. By leaning on God's promises and seeking His strength, you can navigate psychological, financial, physical, and spiritual challenges.

Reflection and Application:

- Reflect on the struggles you face and how you can apply biblical truths to overcome them.
- Identify specific actions you can take to seek God's help and support in each area of struggle.
- Pray for God's guidance and strength as you commit to these practices.

Remember, overcoming struggles is a lifelong journey. Continue to seek God and strive to grow in your faith every day.

Emotional Struggles

Emotional struggles like anger, loneliness, and grief can deeply affect one's spiritual and personal well-being.

1. **Anger**: Learning to manage anger in a healthy, God-honoring way.
   - **Scripture**: "In your anger do not sin: Do not let the sun go down while you are still angry, and do not give the devil a foothold." (Ephesians 4:26-27)

Advice:

- **Practice Forgiveness**: Regularly practice forgiving others to prevent anger from taking root.
- **Seek God's Peace**: Pray for God's peace to calm your anger and give you patience.
- **Find Healthy Outlets**: Engage in activities that help release tension and manage anger healthily, like exercise or talking with a trusted friend.

2. **Loneliness**: Feeling isolated or disconnected from others.
   - **Scripture**: "The Lord is near to the brokenhearted and saves the crushed in spirit." (Psalm 34:18)

Advice:

- **Connect with Community**: Make an effort to connect with your church community or join a small group.
- **Cultivate Relationships**: Invest time in building and maintaining meaningful relationships.
- **Lean on God**: Remember that God is always with you, even in times of loneliness. Spend time in prayer and worship to feel His presence.

3. **Grief**: Dealing with the loss of a loved one or significant change.
   - **Scripture**: "Blessed are those who mourn, for they will be comforted." (Matthew 5:4)

Advice:

- **Allow Yourself to Grieve**: Give yourself permission to grieve and feel the emotions associated with loss.
- **Seek Support**: Reach out to friends, family, or grief support groups for comfort and understanding.
- **Find Hope in Christ**: Hold on to the hope of eternal life and the comfort that comes from knowing your loved ones are with God.

Relational Struggles

Relationships with family, friends, and others can sometimes be challenging and require God's wisdom to navigate.

1. **Family Conflicts**: Managing conflicts within the family.
   - **Scripture**: "If it is possible, as far as it depends on you, live at peace with everyone." (Romans 12:18)

Advice:

- **Practice Patience and Understanding**: Be patient and try to understand the perspectives of your family members.
- **Communicate Effectively**: Use clear and respectful communication to resolve conflicts.
- **Pray for Reconciliation**: Pray for God's guidance and for reconciliation in strained relationships.

2. **Friendship Issues**: Dealing with misunderstandings and conflicts with friends.
   - **Scripture**: "A friend loves at all times, and a brother is born for a time of adversity." (Proverbs 17:17)

Advice:

- **Be Forgiving**: Be quick to forgive and seek forgiveness to maintain strong friendships.
- **Show Love and Support**: Demonstrate love and support in practical ways to strengthen your friendships.
- **Seek Wise Counsel**: If a friendship issue is complex, seek advice from a trusted Christian mentor or pastor.

Vocational Struggles

Challenges in one's career or calling can impact personal and spiritual well-being.

1. **Job Loss**: Coping with unemployment or job transitions.
    - **Scripture**: "And we know that in all things God works for the good of those who love him, who have been called according to his purpose." (Romans 8:28)

Advice:

- **Trust God's Provision**: Trust that God will provide for your needs during times of job loss.
- **Seek New Opportunities**: Actively seek new job opportunities and be open to where God may be leading you.
- **Use the Time Wisely**: Use the time of unemployment to grow in your faith, volunteer, or develop new skills.

2. **Workplace Stress**: Managing stress and challenges at work.
    - **Scripture**: "Come to me, all you who are weary and burdened, and I will give you rest." (Matthew 11:28)

Advice:

- **Take Care of Yourself**: Ensure you are getting enough rest, exercise, and relaxation.
- **Set Boundaries**: Set healthy boundaries to balance work and personal life.
- **Rely on God**: Pray for strength and wisdom to handle workplace challenges and stress.

Spiritual Disciplines

Developing and maintaining spiritual disciplines can help sustain you through various struggles.

1. **Bible Study**: Deepening your understanding of God's Word.
    - **Scripture**: "Your word is a lamp for my feet, a light on my path." (Psalm 119:105)

Advice:

- **Regular Study**: Set aside regular time each day for Bible study.
- **Join a Group**: Join a Bible study group to learn from others

and gain different perspectives.
- **Apply the Word**: Seek to apply biblical principles to your daily life.
2. **Prayer Life**: Enhancing your prayer life.
   - **Scripture**: "Devote yourselves to prayer, being watchful and thankful." (Colossians 4:2)

Advice:

- **Daily Prayer**: Make prayer a daily habit and set aside specific times for it.
- **Pray Scripture**: Use scriptures in your prayers to align your requests with God's will.
- **Prayer Journal**: Keep a prayer journal to record your prayers and note how God answers them.
3. **Worship**: Engaging in meaningful worship.
   - **Scripture**: "God is spirit, and his worshipers must worship in the Spirit and in truth." (John 4:24)

Advice:

- **Personal Worship**: Spend time in personal worship through singing, prayer, and reflection.
- **Corporate Worship**: Participate in corporate worship services to join with others in praising God.
- **Live a Life of Worship**: Seek to live a life that honors God in all that you do, recognizing that worship is more than just singing; it's a lifestyle.

Conclusion

Life as a Christian includes facing and overcoming various struggles. By relying on God's Word, seeking His guidance, and practicing spiritual disciplines, you can navigate these challenges and grow in your faith.

Final Reflection and Application:

- **Reflect on Struggles**: Take time to reflect on the struggles you face in your life.
- **Apply Biblical Principles**: Identify how you can apply the

biblical principles and advice provided in this book to your situation.
- **Seek God's Strength**: Continuously seek God's strength and guidance through prayer, Bible study, and fellowship with other believers.

Remember, overcoming struggles and growing in your faith is a lifelong journey. Continue to seek God, trust in His promises, and strive to live out your faith every day.